e

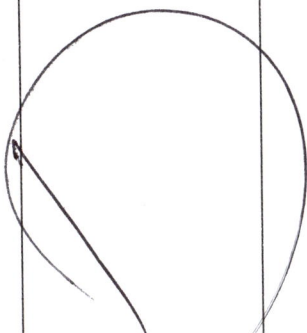

Sheffield
City Council

Renew this item at:
http://library.sheffield.gov.uk
or contact your local library

LIBRARIES, ARCHIVES & INFORMATION

'Vampire Snail'
An original concept by Jenny Moore
© Jenny Moore 2021

Illustrated by Beatriz Castro

Published by MAVERICK ARTS PUBLISHING LTD

Studio 11, City Business Centre, 6 Brighton Road,

Horsham, West Sussex, RH13 5BB

© Maverick Arts Publishing Limited November 2021

+44 (0)1403 256941

A CIP catalogue record for this book is available at the British Library.

ISBN 978-1-84886-837-3

Maverick
publishing
www.maverickbooks.co.uk

Lime

This book is rated as: Lime Band (Guided Reading)

Vampire Snail

written by
Jenny Moore

Illustrated by
Beatriz Castro

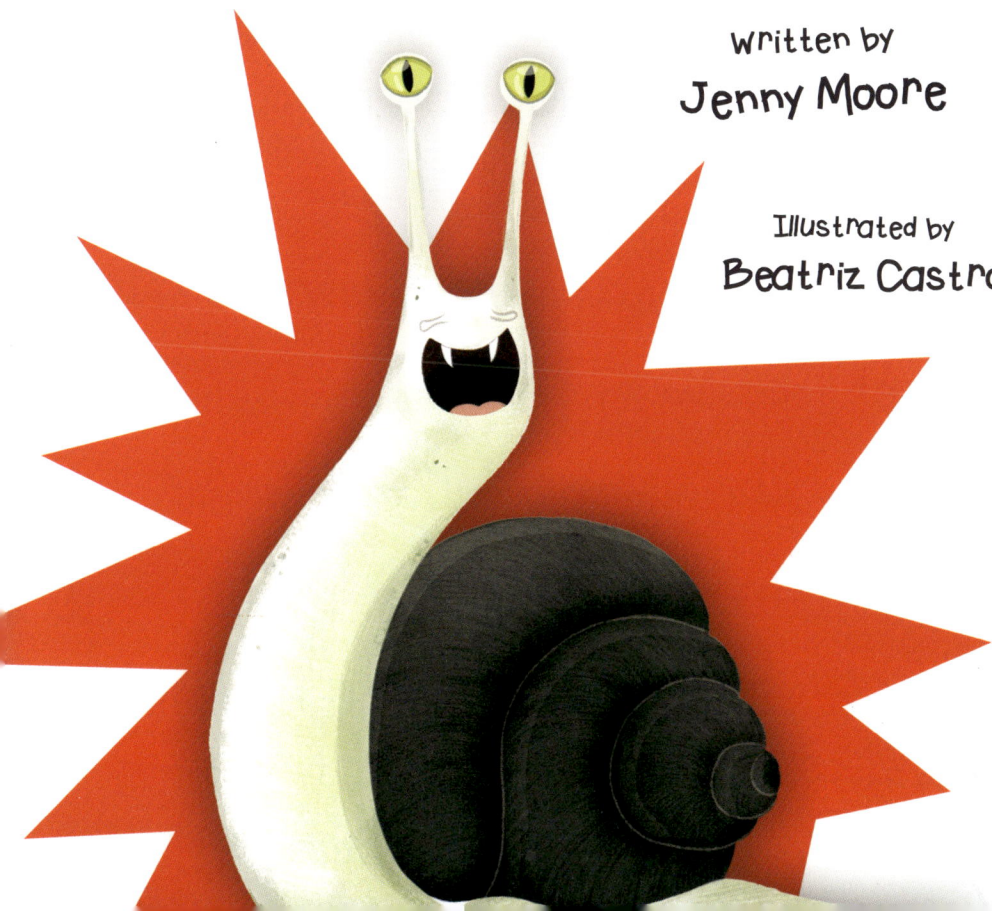

Chapter 1

Jasmin loved Wednesdays. She loved Miss Buffy's after-school nature club. She loved stopping off at the baker's for a treat on the way home. And she loved settling down on the sofa with her new stick insect, Twiggy, to watch her favourite TV shows: *Vanessa Vampire* and *Brilliant Beasts*.

Vanessa wasn't like other vampires. She was a vegetarian animal-lover, who looked after sick

VANESSA VAMPIRE

bats and drank red grape juice instead of blood. She was also a black belt in karate! Jasmin was a big Vanessa fan.

Jasmin was a big fan of Bibi Bugg from *Brilliant Beasts* too. Bibi knew everything there was to know about bugs and slugs and snails. This week she was talking about a giant blue snail that had been discovered in the Amazon rainforest.

"This isn't just *any* snail," said Bibi, looking excited. Its body was a beautiful blue colour. "It doesn't hide away when it feels threatened. It pokes its head out and spits at its enemies instead! That's why I'm wearing this special protective mask."

Wow! thought Jasmin. *That's so cool! I wish I could discover a rare new snail.*

"The Blue Spitting snail has an enormous appetite too," said Bibi. "It can eat a whole melon in a single day!"

Jasmin remembered the leftover melon sitting in the fridge. Mum had sliced it up for fruit salad the night before, but hadn't needed it all. Maybe Jasmin could use it to attract some more exotic creatures to Dad's vegetable patch.

"It's time for you to go back in your cage," she told Twiggy, when *Brilliant Beasts* had finished. "I'm going snail hunting!"

Chapter 2

Jasmin fetched the spare melon from the fridge and grabbed a torch out of the shed. Then she set off through the garden with a torch to begin her search.

There were already plenty of snails feasting on Dad's vegetables. They were just normal brown ones though. Jasmin put down some chunks of melon and waited to see what happened.

Nothing—that's what happened. She waited and waited but there was no sign of any exotic new snails. Even the brown snails weren't interested. They were too busy enjoying Dad's lettuces.

Jasmin put some more chunks down by the flowerbed. A few ants came along to investigate but no colourful new snails. It was the same story over by the apple tree. Perhaps the melon was a bad idea. Jasmin decided to head back inside. She went to put the torch back in the shed.

Wait, what was that down there by the fence?

Something black and shiny glinted in the torchlight. Something big, black and shell-shaped!

It wasn't a Spitting Blue snail, but it *was* an exciting discovery! Jasmin had never seen a snail like him before. His body was pure white, with bright yellow eyes. There was something strange about his mouth too. Jasmin bent down for a closer look. She gasped out loud as the snail lifted his head to reveal two long fangs! Wow! A vampire snail! How cool was that?

She fetched the old fish tank out of the garage, filling it with lettuce and cabbage leaves and the last few bits of melon. The snail curled back into his shell and Jasmin lifted him gently into the tank. The feeding hole cover in the lid was missing, but hopefully the snail would be too busy munching to try and escape.

"It won't be for long," she promised. "I want to take you into school tomorrow to show Miss Buffy. I bet *she's* never seen a vampire snail before either!"

Jasmin carried the tank upstairs to her bedroom and put it next to the stick insect cage.

"Look," she told Twiggy. "I've found you a new friend. I need you to keep an eye on him, and make sure he doesn't crawl off in the night.

Don't worry, he's not as scary as he looks. He's a

vegetarian vampire, like Vanessa! At least I *hope*

he is..."

Chapter 3

Jasmin woke up early the next morning, feeling worried. What if her rare new snail had slithered away in the night? She jumped out of bed to check on him, pressing her nose up against his tank and peering inside. *Phew!* He was still there!

"Good morning," she said, grinning through the glass at him. "How are you today?"

The snail's eyes swivelled on their long stalks as if he was watching her. He bared his fangs.

"I hope you didn't scare Twiggy with those big vampire teeth of yours," said Jasmin. She turned to the stick insect cage and gasped out loud. The lid was open. "Twiggy? Oh no, what's happened?"

Jasmin stared at the remains of her stick insect, still clinging to her stick. It looked like someone—or some*thing*—had sucked Twiggy dry, leaving nothing but a hollow, empty husk. The vampire snail must have escaped out of his tank and into Twiggy's cage, then attacked her in the middle of the night.

"What did you do to her?" asked Jasmin, fighting back tears. "Poor Twiggy." But the snail had already shrunk back inside his shell. Maybe he *wasn't* a nice vegetarian vampire after all.

Chapter 4

Jasmin fixed some cardboard and tape over the feeding hole in the tank lid. She didn't want the snail escaping again. Then she carried it carefully into school to show Miss Buffy.

"Oh yes," said Miss Buffy, peering through the glass. "That *is* unusual. I don't think I've seen a black snail before."

"That's just his shell," said Jasmin. "His body's white, with yellow eyes and big fangs. I think he's a vampire."

Miss Buffy laughed. "I've heard of vampire bats," she said. "I've even heard of bloodsucking birds called vampire ground finches. But I've never heard of a vampire snail."

"It's true," said Jasmin. "He attacked my stick insect. Poor Twiggy was nothing but a dried-out husk when I found her this morning."

"Are you sure that was Twiggy?" asked Miss Buffy. "Stick insects shed their skins when they're growing. Maybe that's what you saw."

Jasmin felt a spark of hope. Could Twiggy still be alive? But she'd checked every inch of her cage and there'd been no sign of her.

Miss Buffy tried to tempt the snail out of his shell with a juicy leaf of lettuce.

"He won't come out now," said Jasmin. "It's too bright. Vampires are allergic to sunlight."

Miss Buffy laughed again. "Perhaps I could take him home to look at tonight, in that case? I'll send some photos to my friend who's a minibeast expert. She might know what kind of snail he is."

"Alright," Jasmin agreed. "But be careful. Watch out for those fangs."

Chapter 5

Jasmin was the first person in the playground the next day. She was desperate to know what Miss Buffy's minibeast expert friend had said. *Was* the new snail a vampire who fed on stick insects? Jasmin had checked and rechecked Twiggy's cage and there was no sign of her.

There was no sign of Miss Buffy either. She was usually out on playground duty when the children arrived. There was no sign of her when Jasmin got to class. It was a supply teacher instead.

Oh no, thought Jasmin. Had the vampire snail bitten Miss Buffy, sucking her dry like poor Twiggy? Or had he turned *her* into a vampire too?

Maybe she was allergic to sunshine as well now...
maybe that's why she wasn't at school.

Jasmin spent all day worrying. She was still worrying on her way home, when she spotted a familiar figure heading into the local shop. It was Miss Buffy! She was looking very pale and wearing dark sunglasses. *That's not a good sign*, thought Jasmin.

She followed Miss Buffy inside. She didn't want to get *too* close though, in case her teacher was a dangerous vampire now. Jasmin hid behind a shelf and peered out. Miss Buffy was at the counter, paying for her shopping. What was she buying? An eye mask to keep out the light? Toothpaste for her new fangs?

"Can I interest you in any of our special offers?" asked the shopkeeper. "It's buy one get one free on garlic bread today."

Jasmin pricked up her ears. According to *Vanessa Vampire*, garlic was bad news for vampires.

Miss Buffy shook her head. "No thank you," she said. "I've gone off garlic lately."

Oh no, thought Jasmin, as a sick feeling of dread washed over her. *I wish I'd never found that horrid snail.*

Chapter 6

Jasmin went straight to her bedroom when she got home, to read up on vampires.

If Miss Buffy really was a vampire now, Jasmin needed to be prepared. Hopefully she'd be a nice, vegetarian one like Vanessa. But what if her teacher had turned into an evil bloodsucker like Dracula?

Jasmin cast a sad look at her empty stick insect cage and then got to work with her vampire reading.

She was so busy reading she didn't hear the knock on the front door. She didn't hear her mum going to answer it. She didn't hear anything until her mum came hurrying up the stairs to find her.

"Jasmin," called Mum, sticking her head round the bedroom door. "Miss Buffy's here to see you."

"M-M-Miss Buffy?" Jasmin repeated, feeling worried. "Wh...what does *she* want?"

"Why don't you go downstairs and find out," Mum said, rubbing at her neck.

Jasmin was *really* worried now. "What's wrong with your neck?" she asked. Had Miss Buffy bitten her? Was Mum a vampire too now?

"It's just a bit sore from playing the violin," said Mum.

Jasmin wasn't sure she believed her. Perhaps *she* should have got some garlic bread from the shop: one stick to fight off Miss Buffy, and one to fight off Mum.

Chapter 7

"Ah, there you are," said Miss Buffy, with a big smile.

Jasmin gave her teacher a long, hard stare. She wasn't wearing sunglasses anymore—that was a good sign. She didn't look as pale as before, and her teeth seemed nice and normal. There was no sign of any fangs.

"Are you alright?" asked Jasmin. "I saw

you in the shop with your sunglasses on, and I thought the snail might have turned *you* into a vampire too."

"A vampire!" Miss Buffy laughed. "I had a bit of a migraine this morning, that's all. That's why I wasn't in school. And that's why I had my dark glasses on when I went to buy some tablets. But they've done the trick. I'm feeling better now."

"Oh," said Jasmin, breathing out a big sigh of relief. *Thank goodness for that.*

"Don't worry, I'm not here to suck your blood," Miss Buffy joked. "I just came to tell you what my friend Bibi Bugg said about your snail."

"Bibi Bugg?" repeated Jasmin. "From *Brilliant Beasts*? I *love* that show."

"Yes, we're old friends," said Miss Buffy. "And she was very interested in your snail. She'd like to take a closer look at him, if that's alright with you? She thinks he might be an undiscovered new species. She's invited you and your snail to come and meet her on the show next Wednesday. How does that sound?"

Wow! It sounded amazing. But Jasmin had just spotted something even *more* amazing crawling across the ceiling above them.

"Twiggy!" she cried. "You're alive!" Miss Buffy must have been right all along. It must have been Twiggy's old skin she'd seen in the cage. The real Twiggy must have pushed open the cage lid herself, and escaped during the night!

"Bibi says they'll be looking at a rare new slug on the show as well,"

said Miss Buffy. "It's called the Yellow Zombie."

Zombie slugs *and* vampire snails? "That sounds brilliant," said Jasmin. She grinned. "I can't wait!"

★★★

It *was* brilliant. Jasmin was a bit nervous at first—she'd never been on television before. But Bibi was so nice and friendly that her nerves soon disappeared.

"Thank you for bringing in your special snail to show us today," said Bibi. "I'm very excited to meet him. We're going to turn the studio lights down low now and see if we can have a proper look at him. Hopefully he'll come out and say hello."

Jasmin bit her lip. What if it was still too bright for him? What if he refused to leave his shell?

But she didn't need to worry. Her vampire snail loved being on television! He crawled around for the cameras, waving his long eyestalks and treating them to a close-up view of his fangs.

"Wow," said Bibi. "Just look at those teeth! I've never seen anything like them! Were you scared he might bite?" she asked.

Jasmin thought about finding Twiggy's shed skin inside her cage. She thought about Miss Buffy's dark glasses and dislike of garlic. She thought about Mum's sore neck and hiding in her bedroom reading up about vampires. "Me?" she said. "Scared? Never!"

Discussion Points

1. What are Jasmin's two favourite TV shows?

2. Where did Jasmin find the vampire snail?

a) In a zoo

b) On a tomato

c) By the fence

3. What was your favourite part of the story?

4. Who did Jasmin think had become a vampire?

5. Why do you think Miss Buffy wanted to send the vampire snail to Bibi Bugg?

6. Who was your favourite character and why?

7. There were moments in the story when Jasmin **jumped to conclusions**. Where do you think the story shows this most?

8. What do you think happens after the end of the story?

Pink
Red
Yellow
Blue
Green
Orange
Turquoise
Purple
Gold
White
Lime
Brown
Grey

Book Bands for Guided Reading

The Institute of Education book banding system is a scale of colours that reflects the various levels of reading difficulty. The bands are assigned by taking into account the content, the language style, the layout and phonics. Word, phrase and sentence level work is also taken into consideration.

The Maverick Readers Scheme is a bright, attractive range of books covering the pink to grey bands. All of these books have been book banded for guided reading to the industry standard and edited by a leading educational consultant.

To view the whole Maverick Readers scheme, visit our website at
www.maverickearlyreaders.com

Or scan the QR code to view our scheme instantly!

Maverick Chapter Readers
(From Lime to Grey Band)

Back in the Game
Written by Jenny Jinks
Illustrated by Zeynep Ozatalay

Spooky Scoops
Written by Alison Donald
Illustrated by Maria Kolker

Secret Spaniel
Written by Antonia Pesenti

Maverick Chapter Readers
Maverick Chapter Readers
Maverick Chapter Readers